Listen...
This is What I Said

A Self-help Guide for Conversations
in Relationships and Marriages

Dorothea Garrett

Contents

Dedication

This book is dedicated to the significant others who allowed me to say these words and took them to heart to receive and respond to them.

Introduction

This book is written specifically for women, and I hope that it will help you envision how vivid and dynamic your relationships can become on all levels. I bless you in your own personal growth as a special woman, fashioned and created as a necessary being upon the Earth. For you who will listen and grow in your communication, who will flourish in relating to others, and who will become abundant in your creativity, there is no limit to you! You will hear from within your heart and use what you have heard, along with your energy, to speak into the lives of others.

These words I have created have helped me to nurture and thrive in my relationships, as well as causing me to become a more confident woman. I am not afraid to speak and to ask for that which makes me happy but I also freely give into the lives of others to help them become all they can be in life.

This book is written for several reasons: I have seen too many failed courtships and marriages. I have seen diminished communication between husband/wife and significant others. I have observed that women have lost the art of speaking into the lives of their significant others. We as women haven't been taught or are too hurt and really don't know how to speak into the lives of our significant other from the beginning of the relationship. Nor do we know how to trust our creativity, to continue to speak into his life throughout dating and marriage. I am so fed up with failing relationships despite all the self-help books available. It appears the self-help books have not made a major dent in marriages staying together, as divorce is skyrocketing. It seems like society gets wiser, but our marriages and dating battles are still being lost. So in this book, I am attempting to appeal to women to get us to examine and revisit how we are communicating with our significant others and husbands from a heartfelt position. I believe if we can stand on what we come to understand as true then we can be in the relationship to win it!!

Some may have that too-cautious feeling that is too afraid to ever trust in another individual. When we meet and are attracted to one another, have the vibes, have a connection and have established that we are in a relationship, then we can begin to really speak to them. Yes, we must know that our efforts won't be in vain or fleeting since this requires work on the part of the woman.

In the ancient text it says:

Thy Word is truth; sanctify thy Word in me; consecrate and dedicate Thy Words so that I may speak them. Allow the Law of Kindness be in our mouths and allow our speech to be seasoned with grace so that it may minister grace to the hearer.

Understand that before reading on, you must be a believer in yourself; you must develop yourself so that you can give of yourself. Gone are the days of maintaining your relationship based upon what you see and feel, since what you see and feel will eventually come to an end without consistent words. I am convinced that you need to know more than you currently know about your significant other or your husband. And who knows them better than their own hearts? The Universe will work in concert with our thoughts, words and feelings. You can speak words, which are things, so that what you say gets through to their hearts and once in the heart, your words will impact them or prompt them to behave in a changed manner.

Here is what I believe, and this has been proven scientifically. If you have a glass of dirty water how do you fill it with clean water so that it is beneficial to you for drinking and refreshing yourself? The answer is you must continually pour clean water into the glass and eventually the dirty water will filter out. The same principle applies when speaking to your significant other. In everything you say you should make an impact upon the heart that will move him to be motivated to act or change. The only true water I know is our "words." Our words carry life or death. Our words can build up or tear down. Our words can cause nations to war or not. Rooted anger and malice cause us to be out of position, and that's why we must look within and deal with ourselves continually. If you will determine to give your significant other a continuous flow of truth and goodness based upon speaking good words into him, you will begin to have knowledge of how he was created so that you can speak to that!

I believe any apparent imperfection can be dealt with since imperfections generate from within the heart of a person. This insight is a powerful point of view and will enable you to speak truth to him. Gone should be the nasty, sniping, vengeful, hurtful words from our mouths. We really want to be in a capable position to hear and speak; thus, being in that position makes us powerful. It makes us graceful and wise women. We want the good, the grace and gladness that comes with a great relationship. We want the peace and comfort that are achievable within our relationships, and they must begin within ourselves.

Our words carry vibrations and life! What a profound statement! We can give into the heart of our significant other and we as women are fit, meet and adaptable to do it. I believe this with all I that am!! Tap into your creative ability; allow your heart and mouth to pour forth good words and watch changes be performed in your union and relationships.

If you will use the creative energy already resident within you to help clean your own heart daily, you will begin to create your relationship anew and have a greater understanding to know what to speak. Speak what you desire into existence. Then the words that flow out of your mouth will agree with your heart. The two, the heart and mouth, must agree in order to be effective. Some of the reasons we as women change are to create our relationships so that we do good works and become kinder and more loving so that we may become successful in living. If you take this book seriously and seek with all your heart, mind, and soul to do this, there are great benefits. He will think he has the only wife or woman on earth that treats him this way. He will feel needed. He will think he is "Superman" and can do anything. He will consistently think of you during the day. He will call you several times a day. He will behave in the manner that your heart desires and you will fill up his empty inward places. After all, isn't this the type of relationship you desire anyway? Speak it into existence!

Two verses of the ancient text that I find interesting are:

Though the fig tree should not blossom and there be no fruit on the vines, though the yield of the olive should fail and the fields produce no food, though the flock should be cut off from the fold and there be no cattle in the stalls,

Yet I will ..., I will rejoice ... Habakkuk 3:17-18

It seems that in life we may come to a place where we feel we have given up a lot emotionally, mentally, physically and financially. Some have given up after a brief relationship, some after 5, 20 or 40+ years. We sometimes find ourselves later in life without a significant other. But this does not have to be the benediction over our lives...to live life alone.

As we live alone and sulk or maintain not needing men attitudes, we have negative heart, mind, body and financial voices speaking:

> From the heart: emotional love, caring and affection; we may have that too-cautious feeling that is too afraid to ever trust in another individual

> From the mind: mental anguish, confusing thoughts, memories that will not fade

> From the body: stressful events, things we'd rather not go through, aloneness and lonely times and not looking fit

From the financial: spending for unplanned events, giving up resources, and having resources taken away

However, this is only self-talk. We cannot love without becoming vulnerable, naked and unashamed. Real love is cautious and will recognize issues but is willing to not be afraid to love again without conditions.

And with all these things the test here says there is nothing left. No figs… nothing to taste sweet in life, no fruit on the vines…nothing to smell sweet or to look forward to harvesting, no olives to trade and sell, barren fields … no crops to sustain living. There is nothing to touch, no flocks and no cattle in the stalls, no food to trade and sell to gain the necessities of life.

However, with all that is gone from what the eyes can see, there is still hope! "Yet I will…" I will hope and have joy… in unseen things! Because hope and joy are our core attributes given at birth. No one can take them so don't surrender them to anyone or anything. Hope and joy… are the foundational things that sustain us through life… even if the natural eyes perceive there is nothing left.

For with hope and joy…joy is multiplied! Never forget who you are because you don't just have hope, you are hope! You don't just have joy, you are joy. Never surrender who you are because your hope and joy are your responsibility. The power for you to be hopeful and joyful lies inherently within yourself. Therefore, your own hope and joy can help to begin a new thing. Life can begin to be sweet and you can love again. Just remember that with hope and joy...you cannot be stilled... hope and joy overflow the cup of life! Even if walking though the valley of the shadows of things unpleasant...in the presence of what seems like "there is nothing left" ...your cup of life overflows!

Your relationship, too, can overflow with love, kindness, gentleness, meekness and strength!

And thus, *Listen...This is What I Said!* was placed in my heart and acted out in my dating relationships. So I am going to tell you what I said and you may use or allow the Universe to provide you with insight, as you observe your mate or significant other, to speak directly with your own words in your conversations. Also, I added a chapter called "The Flame," which are my dates' responses back to me. They are beautiful words that all women want to hear, and it helps us to flourish in living.

I salute you as women and trust that as you grow, so will your relationships!!

Chapter 1
This is what I said to the Spiritual Son

You are doing well.

There is a season for everything...a time to heal...a time to break down...a time to build up... a time to weep ... a time to laugh... a time to keep ... a time to cast away... In every season of our lives we remember we have hope!!!

Young Man, this is the day designed with your season in mind...unlike any other day, this is your time...live and use what you possess to give this day a brand new you. You are in the mourning state of the past and this is to be expected. There is now, right now, a fresh new day to grow. Don't beat yourself up. It's an experience and the next moment can change.

Since you were not fulfilled, since you are unhappy or unsatisfied...yes, there is pain but it can change. Speak words of life to yourself as I do.

You will NOT allow yourself to be torn apart. You will permit yourself to come into wholeness and healing in every area of your life, and especially through a breakup. When you are stronger, you will stop listening to the anguished thoughts. I know you will emerge stronger.

You feel vulnerable because your emotions are running wild. You are not alone, and I am standing with you!! People do what they do because they do not know what they are doing or how to really love.

Allow these positive words to enter the deep places of your heart where you have carried hurt and pain for all these years. Allow them to restore your joy! Your joy can be restored because it is ever-present, only diminished. You will enjoy the rest of your day!

I am thankful that we abide in safety, even though we walk through hurtful, painful experiences. We are resilient people. In this day let's rejoice in all the good, goodness favor and present love we have. The day awaits your abiding presence.

You are created good! You were born perfect! You can do good works! When we do well it expands our capacity to be better than who we were previously. Goodness and mercy follow us and we are designed to see and live good days. I am so glad that good energy resides within us. I am thankful for you; you are a prince among men. Your day awaits your directions!

You are a righteous man,
You are an overcomer,
You strive to be your best in character,
You have morals and are principled,
You are proficient in professionalism,
You are direct in issue resolution,
You are colorful in laughter, so engaging in conversation,
Rhythmical in performance—yes...You are amazing...
And it is my great pleasure to honor...You!
What was the Creative Energy thinking on the day you came forth?
How you were carefully and skillfully formed,
Infused with love, light, and being. I pause and think!
What was the Creative Energy thinking... placing you upon the earth?
And then... I came forth! Infused with love, light, and being. I pause and think!
I just wonder... what was the Creative Energy thinking?
Our paths crossed...was it planned? Was it destined? Was it skillfully crafted?
That the two should have an encounter that neither would ever forget?
Oh, what was the Creative Energy thinking? Distinctively You!

And by the way...your mind is too anointed to be "dumb" ... if you remember anything I have said to you... always recall to your mind that... YOU ARE A SON!

You are a conquering son! After all, everything flows from the heart! This is what I see in your heart... charitable, kind, and compassionate. You are tempered... forbearing, gentle, and merciful. You are humble... unpretentious, meek, and peaceful. You are full of courage... a warrior, more than a conqueror...able to take back your heart! Be found trusting... for with trust there is a lifting up... raised high above dangers seen and unseen. Praying for you always!

You are a wise son! You have entered into the house of wisdom! Yes, Wisdom favors You! Yayyyyyyy!! You are learning and remaining teachable. You have wisdom, knowledge and understanding; these are your pals. You all look good together! May wisdom reign in you as you live to give... these are words to live by!

You are a wise son! You have the favor within your life. May You always be blessed with length of days, and years of life and peace.

You are a favored son. You received discipline, correction and reproof and you are willing to look within yourself to become better.

You are a favored son! You walk securely; May You always be blessed so that you are not afraid—no calamity in your life and no destruction. You acknowledge your errors and shortcomings. You are a favored son! You are full of wisdom and winning in honor...You are a favored son!

You are a graceful son! You reveal your heart in our relationships and I am mindful of the healing and restoring that is taking place. We walk in peaceful paths...we act with dignity and grace... we guard our hearts and we are known. Young Man... you are being renewed and restored in your life... Life is guiding you into peaceful paths... You are blessed with wisdom to respond with dignity and grace. What a "graceful" son you are!!

You are a wise son! You do not have an argumentative spirit but possess a spirit of agreement (a place of power). You are not a person of strife but rather one who seeks to resolve issues. You are not a person of slander but an encouragement to others. You are not an unfriendly person but one who places a high value on friendships. You speak pleasant words, understanding that life and death are in the words of your tongue. Your heart is not hateful but loving, gentle, and kind...doing good works. War over your heart and be found wise...

You are a hopeful son! I have written to you valuable and treasured words, words of good counsel and knowledge so that you, Young Man, will know that my words are certainly true. When you are strengthened, then you can strengthen others. It's all about words; words that encourage and build up... not words that tear down... words that heal and bind up...not words that cause sickness and brokenness but rather words that infuse hope and not words that bring hopelessness. What is in a word? Life and death are in the power of the tongue...I choose life...the words of life...so you can live, really live!

You are a wise son! You're a man becoming wiser, instructed and laying a firm hold on knowledge. You pursue righteous acts and are kind and faithful. You are beginning to live... really live as never before! Your life is blessed, and you possess riches and integrity, producing good character. No one will be able to stand against your life...it just cannot happen! I am sooo glad that I am here to see the beauty magnified in your life!

You are a good son! You possess a good and kind heart; love, affection, hopes, dreams and fears are deeply embedded within. Not to worry, as you walk, life's energies will enlighten and illuminate your thoughts. And your thoughts and actions will bring you into your destiny. I am so pleased that I have an opportunity to walk through this part of your life with you...always grateful for each opportunity!!

You are a good son! You were created good; you have a good heart and you love deeply. Oh, taste the freedom to love...it's good for you and good to you. I am committed to walking with you through this point in life!

You are a blessed son! You are a very blessed man and there is no need of fear or lack in your life. You are not forsaken! Remember this: even if you fall, a just man will arise because of who he is connected to. And you are connected to all creative energies. And the added favor is that you have someone in your life to demonstrate love...all for you and for years to come!

You are a truthful son! The goal for all of us is maturing in the experiences of life. We come to understanding through our experiences and we determine truth by them. We are made, created, and formed into love—free to be, speak, and do good! Never forget who you are...a son of truth, walking in the good Way, and living the good Life. It is my pleasure to know you!

You are a good son! I see you unmovable...honest in your endeavors...not hurting others...holding fast to your words...and a heart full of honor. You perform good works and everything you set your hands to do shall succeed. You shall not be moved!

You are a courageous son! Be courageous, Young Man... it is pleasant that you walk into a good, successful life.

And I am thankful to be included in the good part of your life. It is my will to be with you in good times and other times...I'll be by your side forevermore!

You are a blessed son! And should you fall...remember a just man may fall but he will arise; you will arise and stand erect. Success and victory are established for you! May this blessing be with you all of your days, just as I will be with you!

You are a joyful son! When you have grieved over lost things—relationships, marriages, apathy, etc.—the Universe hears your heart! Sometimes we dare speak our desires and the Universe answers. It is like the energies and the vibrational sounds of our hearts turn our mourning into delight. Now, it is with joy that you will continue to live...all the days of your life. Baby, you are the sound of my heartbeat and my joy!

You are a Son of favor! Only good days, living far above any circumstances, only love and mercy following you! Only favor dripping like rain in your life. For good will stay with you for as long as you live. Therefore, I will imitate the good...to only do good to you all the days of your life! So I will speak to my soul and say, "Blessed are You, Young Man."

You are a kind-hearted son! Great is my love to and for you, and I am excited about my great treasure. My treasure is you...you are the melody of my heart song... what a precious treasure you are. I am joyful and excited, and I am thankful for the great kindness that has been demonstrated to you and me!

You are a unique son! This is very exciting news! I get to be in a relationship with a uniquely customized man, and I get my instructions for loving You from your heart as you relate with me. This is what I see!

You are a chosen son! That which you have received, you give.... great, great love and kindness. You are chosen and called into love, favor, and kindness...so receive it! It is my pleasure to know you, and it is my greater pleasure to walk through life with You!

You are a loved son! On your path in life, you will encounter your call that has been strategically prepared for you. You will come into understanding life so that you may comprehend and function well in all your work. This is a day like no other; rejoice and be glad in it. After all, you are richly blessed and highly favored! You are loved more than you can ever imagine.

You are a precious son! You are cherished and priceless. Man, you are very treasured and priceless...no one can ever replace the unique You that was precisely timed for a love like mine.

You are a unique son! You are fashioned by great workmanship! What an awesome man you are!! Sometimes when I ponder your Fine Chocolate image, your smile, your stature, it just takes my breath away. Have a marvelous day!

You are a carried son! When you pass through the circumstances of life, look within and renew yourself! This renewing will bring about restoration, guidance, enlightenment, love and these will carry you even until your last day.

You are a sweet son! You are sweeter than bubble gum, sweeter than a Snickers bar...sweeter than honey in coffee...sweeter than an Oreo cookie...all because you are satisfied... Oh, taste and see that this man is good...I have!

The guided son: He guides you with truth and teaches you in the way you should go...His salvation becomes your hope, and what a miraculous hope you have. It doesn't matter where you are...He has already been there for you and provided all you need. By the Spirit of our Creator... He lives in me. And I am fashioned...prepared and made ready for you... Be blessed and rejoice. Live, laugh, and love this day...every good thing waits for you!

Blessed son: Oh, give thanks to our Creator for He is good, and His love for Man never ends... Praise our Creator and I give You thanks and adoration for young Man!!!

Nurturing son: We need our faith now to believe our Creator for your seed in the earth, to give Him a righteous seed back through our children. It will take great faith so we go through this time of faith and move into believing him for twins. We will need to believe that He is a rewarder of those who diligently seek after Him. If He wants life to occur in my womb, then it will…believe and have faith for it.

Timely son: The season and timing of your life was a marvelous plan, a magnificent novel waiting for your presence upon the earth so that you could live out the plan. It took accurate timing, planning and preparation. Then the announcement… "Man is birthed into the earth." You were born at the right time, in the right place, in the right race, placed into the right family, and you are not a coincidence! Your anticipated arrival was uniquely calculated…now you live out His plan for your life. What a treasure you are, prepared for this moment in time, raised up for this life, this love, this linking together…you…our Creator…and me. What a perfect connection and a winning combination. Peradventure we were born for such a time as this…to fulfill this destiny. Some people wait a lifetime for a moment like this…behold the good thing that has been placed before us…

Loved Son: You are so loved it is unfathomable! Our Creator secured His love for you before there was an earth and before there was even the first Adam. Our

Creator sent His unique Son, our Messiah, to be your deliverer and salvation, but it is so much more. He secured love, grace, mercy and eternal life for you! His love is good, great, and gracious to you. Along with His love is healing…healing for your mind, body and spirit. And out of His vast love we are forgiven and delivered from destruction. Praise His Name! Just like our Creator, you have sent your love to me and I have sent my love to you! It's a great time to know one another and be in the moment…after all…love is all it is….

Here is the good and excellent news…Our Creator announced from the beginning of your existence that His plan would hold fast and He would do everything He pleased to do within your life! Always remember…your life was established from the beginning and no one, no thing, and no circumstance can ever cause His plans for you not to work for your good, even things not yet seen in the earth. All things are accomplished for you at His pleasure, and you are well-pleasing to Him. There is a peace I have come to know that while everything else may look awry, there is an anchor for my soul, where I can say, "It is well." Why? Because everything He pleases has already been announced for our lives…

Restored son: Love is the most powerful force in the heavens and on the earth…for it is out of our Creator's love that we are restored to health and healed of wounds: emotional, mental, physical, etc. He declares that He will perform your restoration to health and He will heal. It doesn't matter how we feel or what others say...It is on the truth of our Creator that we are restored! We are grateful that in all things He cares for us. I am excited and it is my prayer that you are always restored in every area of your life. You are a good man possessing a good heart... be prosperous and blessed in all you put your hands to do this day!

Glorious son: Love is the most powerful force upon the earth...and you see love is not just in word but demonstrated in deeds. It is with immeasurable love that our Creator demonstrates His love to us. Our Creator declares that it won't be long and He will shake the heavens, earth, sea, dry land, and all the nations...a tremendous shaking for our sakes! It will be a shaking that produces complete glory in us; we are His precious people and we carry a great treasure within us...You possess great grace and love... making us a powerhouse of glory. After all, we are the temple of our Creator. Our glory is greater than our past; it's already done! He spoke His Word from the foundation of the earth. What an unfathomable love toward us! Our new frame and stature is of a grandee nature and we surpass any and everything that has happened in our past. We possess our Creator's peace! You are a "powerhouse" of glory...So glad you are on the planet!

Chapter 2
This is what I said to the Nurtured Son

I really miss you! I feel like part of myself is missing; I am so happy you feel that way about missing me.

Good night, my love...not enough wine on the planet. How do I breathe without you?

Good morning, my love. Baby, I love you, I need you, I want you and I desire only you. It is my determination, desire and destiny to make You feel so special, so wanted...my priority. You have a love unlike anything else; that love causes you to have an amazing life.

Good morning, my Chocolate Kiss, my love.

No greater love has a man than that he will lay down his life for his friend. This is such a GREAT LOVE! Great love flowing from me into you and from you into me! What an awesome love affair! And my life is submitted to you, all for you...

This is for real, forever, for all your lifetime...Isn't it wonderful? Moment by moment we freely yield our love one to another. Your day awaits all the love you can give.

Better now. Are you okay? Since all is well with you then I am elated!

Yes, like the nectar of your love! You and your innocent love are young, and you should blush! I hope to keep you blushing...endlessly!

Okay baby...just anticipating seeing you! I loved my company and the lunch! Thank you...I still smell you!

I was addressing moving on from a relationship that was not working; I had to move on from that as a kindness to the other person. It is not in my will to leave, forsake, move on, or go away from YOU! I believe in an "Us" in due time. And like you told me: "And I will stay"—not run but stay. Baby, it is my will, my willingness to stay with you.

I just love you and how you think! I will be delighted to hear you call me that name. What an extremely awesome kindness you have shown to me in this already blissful day! The package of gloves arrived, and I just cannot fathom how perfect they are in taste, size, color, and style.

You are my precious treasure extraordinaire! Thank you for caring for my hands and their being warm and chic. I'm simply speechless!

Thank you for trusting me with your heart...I will take it and love all the pain away, and do it patiently and fervently, with the passion you so deserve. Baby, I love my Chocolate Kiss.

You are a good man, a wonderful tapestry full of the same goodness, grace and grandeur as you have been created with! Weave a good day for yourself.

I want to honor you in this matter. I don't want you to feel guilty or anything like that. You have enough to deal with now. I can wait.

Thank you for being so gracious, honest and kind to me. I will love you forever!

You have given me an open invitation that does not expire. I feel so blessed and thankful that you have placed your heart in my trust...I will be very guarded with your heart!

You and I are both safe at home, and that warms my heart. Please be safe; you carry my precious man, my Chocolate Kiss. I miss you now! Enjoy your friends and return safely, my love. My love goes with you; my heart is knitted together with yours.

Beloved son: Allow me to recall to your remembrance who you are:

You are a favored son,
You are a wise son,
You are an exalted son,
You are an honored son,
You are graced son,
You are a glorious son,
You are a blessed son,
You are a known son,
You are a righteous son,
You are a healed son,
You are a restored son,
You are a courageous son,
You are a raised-high son,
You are a well-versed son
You are a thoughtful son,
You are a guided son,
You are a freed son,
You are a peaceful son,
You are a treasured son,

You are a beloved son...my, my.... how astoundingly loved you really are!

Chapter 3:

This is what I said to the Sexy Son - My Lover, my Husband

As I ponder you, smiling,
As I remember you, pleasing,
As I read you, happy,
As I envision you, excited—
Just You!

A winning attitude,
An eye-pleasing build,
A wonderful smile,
A brilliant mind…all these and more you possess,
Being a man unlike any other…indescribably You!

We strive to be the greatest part of ourselves...loving one another!

Song: *"Night and day, you are the one, only you 'neath the moon or under the sun,*
Whether near to me or far, it's no matter, darling, where you are; I think of you day and night."

Do this...while it's daylight, go outside...
Look up toward the sun, see its rays and enjoy the warmth it gives.
Observe the blue sky and whether there are any clouds.
Why? I see the same sun, I see the same rays, and I enjoy the same warmth.
Do this......at nighttime go outside...
Look up at the moon and stars; see the bright lights.
Observe the twinkling stars; tell me what you see.
Why? I see the same moon and stars; I see the same dark sky.
We live in the same Universe, under the same sky...
I may be observing the same constellation you see...
Darling, I am right outside looking, as you are...
I keep looking up...that's where I find one miraculous You!

At the thought of You., I am enchanted!
At the sound of You., I anticipate!
At the scent of You, I awaken!
At the sight of You, I live!

At the touch of You, I tremble!
At the taste of You, I am delighted!
Only You!

Sun, moon, stars…Creator's gifts.
Gold, silver, diamonds…prized baubles.
Glass, china, pewter…beautiful decorations.
You then; You now; and You will always be… cherished treasure!

Know this…if a significant other does not see you, provide unfeigned love, serve you, adore and cherish you… then what's the point?

As the pen crafts inspiring words,
As emotions generate positive vibrations,
As a heart produces the rhythmic beat,
So the Creative Energy at the apex of creativity astoundingly created You!
And I am so grateful!

Oh, Heavens pour out your joy;
Oh, Earth bring forth your dew;
Oh, Wind breathe on me;
There is a command in the atmosphere that is unmistakably…You!

I am writing this so that you have it as law and for reference in your personal law library.

May I remind you that you cannot have a nightmare or bad dream and call me that I would not be there. We both cannot forget what we started and what we share… Know this assuredly…if you call, I will come…. "I'll be there to catch you; whenever you call!" It is only a mere flight.

Dark, red, vivid…beets.
Dark, blue, sweet…blueberries.
Dark, red, juicy…grapes.
Dark…vivid…sweet…and juicy…YOU!

Day make your dawning! A brand-new day!
Wake up, Sun! Shine intensely!
Spread, blue sky! Vividly and vivaciously!
He's coming…he's stirred…he's up!
What a perfect and flawless day…You are here!

Dark and deep eyes…you possess;
An eye-pleasing face…you possess;
A sensational smile that lights up the soul,
Arms that embrace, arms that hold…you possess;
Hands that touch and comfort…. you possess;
Strong legs that support you on your constitutional stroll…you possess.
Dark in hue…sweet in emotion…lustrous in elegance…. a delectable treasure.
Yes, these I do remember…etched in my soul…yes, these…are just the way You are!

I looked up at the darkened sky and all the stars were shining in their array, glittering, brilliant, and gleaming in their splendor and luminous energy. Then I gazed upon a radiant picture of you...fine physique, handsome and statuesque, poised and stately. Those stars...Oh my, how they pale in comparison to you...they envy you...wishing they could be You!

Wake up, sun! Yay!
Wake up, stars! Yippee!
Applaud the day...He is here and welcomed! Wow!

I had a dream in which I was being cared for by an honorable gentleman. He was kind, thoughtful, and undeniably wild about me. He permeated every area of my life...I ate delectably from his table and this was his unquenchable desire. We were inseparable...sweating and breathing very hard, I awakened. I shook myself and consciously I smiled. That dream was my reality in...unquestionably You! Go ahead, blush; I wonder how it must feel to know that you are my dream come true.

You see into who I really am; and you allow me the ultimate pleasure of using this treasured gift upon you. My, my, what a wise and perceptive man you are!

I saw a beautiful, picturesque morning sunrise, then I remembered an equally picturesque, handsome son rise...... You!

Wake up, sun! Yay!
Wake up, stars! Yippee!
Applaud the day...He is here and welcomed! Wow!

This is a sensational day just because you are in it!!!
Peace...no matter what happens...just know that I am standing with you.
You will have a wonderful life; I just know it. No need to respond...I am good.

Just as morning follows evening and day follows night,
As the stars present their light in radiant array,
Their light for us to see that they are present and accounted for,
Glittering as they were established to give pleasant sight...
Just as the love we share between us,
Is displayed brightly; your love looks so good on me,
Beaming with the same love that I was designed to give,
For all to see that I am present and counted in with you...
Smile and have a radiant day...
I will be loving You...always!

One year ago we began an interesting conversation over lunch and decided to move in a direction of "we".
One year ago we began to move into discovery and finding out who we were...
One year ago we began to think in terms of a future, perpetuity, endless...

Along the way we found out that Snickers bars, Oreo cookies and BUBLE GUM were our favorites...

Along the way we found out that we liked to eat, pray, laugh, and talk about anything and everything...together.

Along the way we saw unique things we liked about each other...gardens, George's, girls, and everything.

Along the way we saw an undisturbed love that was still intact...even though we have experienced similar hurts...

Along the way we fell into a unique love...a priceless love...

Along the way we saw that we perfectly reflected each other's lives...

Now, one year later...we are moving around each other's hearts...

Now, one year later...we are still laughing, talking, sharing...

Now, one year later...we believe in endless love...we believe in forever...

Now, one year later...we continue...

Love is the most powerful force upon the earth......and you see, love is not just in word but demonstrated in deeds. Our Creator loves us. What an awe-inspiring love toward us! You see, anyone can love the lovely but the real true test of love is loving while things are in progress—loving through issues, loving through awkward situations, loving through hurt, loving through faith, and loving through being treated unkindly. When love is tried and tested and one can endure and still love...that's loving just like our Father. This is called abiding, staying inside, and enduring love. I believe this is the love we are working toward and shall obtain.

I see your love in your deeds and...
It's loving like our Messiah...redeeming us through laying down His life for another.
It's loving like Boaz...willing to minister to every hunger Ruth had (physical, etc.).
It's loving like Abraham...willing to listen to Sarah's words and do as she asked.
It's loving like Esther's King Ahasuerus...never refusing her presence, always receiving her.
And in the words of Stevie Wonder...I'll be loving you always!

Love is the most powerful force upon the earth...loving like the Source is a lasting, enduring, never-ceasing love. For the Source loved you so greatly...you are accepted in the Beloved! Love saves, delivers, redeems and restores us back into truth. The Source bears us up and will never let us down. His love is patient and kind...never ending. What an absolutely amazing, precious love He has toward you and His children. Man, I love you and only hope that I can fulfill this scripture in our time. I have faith/trust, hope, and love...and the greatest thing a man or woman can possess is...a willing heart to love.

May the Source bless you and keep you — may He speak well of you and do you good all the days of your life.

May the Source make His face shine on you and show you His favor — may you always live in His presence, know He is guiding you, and all favors and gifts abound toward you.

May the Source lift up His face toward you — may you always look toward Jerusalem and may He always behold your life.

And May the Source give you His peace — may your life prosper where He is passionate about nothing missing, nothing lacking, and nothing broken in your life! All things restored!

Unhindered son: You live life and love others…all in the presence of our Creator. He walks within your thoughts, emotions, and actions and calls you to be His son. He assures you that when you walk among your thoughts and emotions that the actions you take will not be hindered, and you won't trip over your footsteps/progress. Further, if your actions cause you to run with your decisions… you will not stumble. What great and precious promises we all have from our Father! You are called to live in His pathways and His Word is a lamp for your feet and a light for your pathway…you will not be stalled, stuck or delayed; you will not blunder, misstep or make a mistake because of the faith you possess in Him and His great love for you to be successful. No hindrances and no stumbling for you!

Righteous son: You and children from the Source are likened to trees; we are called oaks/trees of righteousness. Our Creator created and planted us from the foundation of the earth to do the works of righteousness. We are declared righteous in the Beloved: Yeshua! So if a tree appears to be cut down, appears to be dying, appears to bear no fruit, yet...at the scent of water it will sprout again and grow. We all have setbacks and setups in life that may weigh us down...but we still possess hope! Then, at the scent of water, the water of His Word, we are enlightened with wisdom and continue to grow in knowledge and understanding. May our Creator supply you today with wisdom, knowledge and understanding for your life...and may you receive all that He provides! You are a mighty oak!

Enlightened son: You have a calling; I have a calling and all of the Source and all children have a calling...called out of darkness into the light of the Source...His enlightenment! He always wants His children to have wisdom, knowledge and an understanding heart, so that we may not perish for lack of wisdom, so that we may know that the Source of all things...the Source which is the Divine and the Power of Powers. You are chosen by Him and called! Your aptly anointed mind is wiser today than yesterday…you possess wisdom beyond your years. May He always provide and may you always receive His light, His Word, His commands, and His supply.

Joyful son: Today, we get another opportunity to live, laugh, and love. This is another moment to rejoice in our hearts because our Creator has provided this time for us. We will rejoice and be glad because we trust and have faith in the Source. Listening to the Source we can accomplish all things—who can stand against us? The Source is a strong tower and the righteous run in and we are safe! You have a joyful heart and allow your mind to comprehend victory in all things. This is your life…your day… your time…. your moment; some people wait a lifetime for love moments like these…rejoice!

May the light of the Source and wisdom fill you up in thought, emotions and body…and regenerate everything that is within you!!

The Good son: Today is a day unlike any other day, unique in the beauty it brings. Today, we trust and live by faith… faith that the Source will bring us to your desired purpose and destiny. While we are at home in our bodies, we must acknowledge the Source who loves us unashamedly, who gives us all good things (every good and perfect thing, and the Source never changes). Remember, our Source is only going to give us good gifts and do good acts. Surely, goodness and mercy will follow you all of your days…

You are a good thing! Oh my, such a good thing you are. Just like the Source of all...

Given the fact that nothing—and no person—is perfect in this life, I see us as being as perfect a couple as humanly possible. We have a lot in common, which is good for both of us; we complement one another very well. Our differences are also good, as they serve to keep us in balance and accountable to each other.

At this point, I don't even want to speculate on my life without you.

Enlightened son: Baby, never fret, or be dismayed.... the Source is your light and He will ensure you are on the righteous path, well illuminated for you to fulfill your calling and so that you are fulfilled in life.

Nurturing son: The Source of all things is willing to protect, guide, guard, and nurture you. And in like manner, I see your behavior in those you nurture, those whom you care for. You protect, guard and give advice to those who are in your circle of influence...including me. I feel safe, secure, and surrounded by love and kindness when I am with you...always wanting to be with you.

Wealthy son: It has been said that where your wealth is or where your treasure is, there your heart will be also. So the question is what is your wealth? I perceive in you that your wealth is the Source, family, friends, health, wisdom, knowledge and understanding. Therefore, your heart is with the right things in life...and you move about the planet in unity, walking in unity and your heart is full, blessed and good. I am so thankful that I get to walk with you. My heart is with you and when I open it unto you, such a wonderful treasure chest of precious things is inside.... real love, laughter, unity, acceptance, desire, understanding and so much more...

Knowing son: I see you desiring to know more, especially in our relationship. This desire will culminate in you knowing and dwelling with me according to knowledge, living with what you know. And I shall know you more and more each day, which will bring about unity and fellowship with each other. You are rising to a higher level of knowledge of yourself and me, just as you are known by the Source and me! You are an honorable man.

Loved son: Welcome to the joy of the Divine Source being complete in you! Welcome to happiness! Welcome to delightfulness and peace! Welcome into favor! Welcome into peace, resolute peace within yourself! And welcome into my love!

Victorious son: You and I desire every good and perfect thing that life has for us and maybe, just maybe, there are some giants in the land. We slay the giants...this is the victory that overcomes, even as we hold fast to our faith.

Let us be steadfast, resolute and unmovable, always willing to show up and go in to take possession of those good and perfect things that only come from the Divine Source within. Remember…you are my good and perfect man.

Receiving son: Do not forget today that you are in a receiving mode, a finding mode, and a going-through-the-door mode. Nothing can stop these events from happening to you…it's all about what you believe and your faith. Let's choose to believe that we receive the good things and that provisions increase for us. You are a good thing, just as I am a good thing! And I receive all of you, including your restored life! We are the restorers of whatever is broken and we restore our life pathways to dwell, live and reside in.

Peaceful son: So good, so gracious, so loving and so kind is life to provide you…a man who is part of the splendor from the Divine Source! A peaceful son…one who fulfills my life, one who will redeem my love and draw that love out from the well of my heart. I am so glad and satisfied that you live and that we get to walk out life together. You are a blessed, peaceful son…

Hospitable son: Thank you for being so hospitable; it shows that you demonstrate love by those you serve. This is how other men will know you: by your love for your brethren. You show great love to your family, your friends, those you worship with, your direct reports and now me. We cannot fathom the world without you in it!

So willing and faithful to help and assist others! Your gift of hospitality will make room for you among great men. Oh, and such a wonderful smile. Your loving service and kindness will be my testimony before others as I reflect you on the earth.

Recovering son: Sometimes we weep in the dark areas of our lives...intrusions which are broken relationships, broken dreams, sick bodies in need of healing, and seemingly no hope. These dark times are only momentary because we are guaranteed that favor lasts a lifetime and joy comes with light, illumination and hearing from the Divine Source; changing our thinking brings light. Rejoice, and again "re"-joy within yourself! I have heard that David recovered all .... rejoicing! We rejoice and we recover all too! The past is just that—the past; we enjoy and rejoice in our present moment, which is our gift. And the favor that lasts a lifetime is so profound that we are eternally grateful.

Mighty son: Young Man, know that your life will have peace, and at times you will have to fight the good fight to maintain your faith. Know that the Divine Source has provided you with a woman who will have your back, as your rear-guard, and that's a good thing. From our conversation, you reminded me of King David's mighty men in how you care for and plan to treat your wife. You possess a wonderful gift in that you have good insight into marriage and what it takes to keep the relationship going. You provide even to the point of sacrifice. You possess a deep, abiding love to share that has been preserved and not quenched. You may even have some fears based on living and loving. My prayer is that you fear not and you vibrate higher! Behold, the Divine Source knows the intimate, specific cravings of your heart; remember you are worthy and deserving of all good things.

Never abandoned son: I love you and will always do my best, knowing that you care for and about what happens to me, as you have demonstrated. I trust and pray that the Divine Source will be our eyes and watch over us as we grow together and help us to be wise in times of unknowing and where we have questions…that we are guided by our faith into a place where it is always safe for us. We are two souls, finding love and growing the love we share, binding ourselves together in love so that our love will guide us in perfect harmony.

Righteous Son: Righteous living is that you are in the right place, doing the right things, at the right time, with the right people, and your heart is in right-standing in the Universe before the Divine Source. It is my firm belief that we were divinely destined to meet. Standing in the right position, in the right place, at the right time with you is our foundation. This love we possess flows right, feels right, and forever will be…after all…everything is from the heart.

Princely son: Thank you for living beyond hurts and frustrations; thank you for your steadfastness to live and to love. You are my "object lesson" on earth and you remind me more and more of the Boaz character each time I am in your presence or speaking with you. Do you know when you say, "You are with me now; you are connected to me" that you are redeeming me and marriage for both of us on the earth? This is all made possible by the crafted timing of the Universe! As Boaz was listed in the Hall of Fame, you will be listed in my Hall of Fame as a great man, a prince among men.

Loving son: You perform as our Creator does by possessing a great love...provisional, nurturing, caring, nourishing, cherishing, and treasuring. You really have a propensity to love, and I am so very glad you are here on this earth! When the Source of all things created you, I am sure the Source of all things was thinking about me!

Sexy son: You, I am thankful just as you are thankful because we are united.
I am thankful that you awakened today with the kiss of life proved by the dimples on your cheeks.
I am thankful that you are the only man on the planet with a passionate love toward me.
I am thankful that you see how to love and display it freely.
I am thankful that you possess eyes to see, ears to hear, and an understanding heart to love others...and me.

I am thankful that you perform in the manner of provision, love, mercy goodness, grace, joy...aaahhh, what a fine and handsome man!
I am thankful that you are not fearful to be who you were fashioned to be...my, my, what a MAN!

Victorious son: Sometimes in life I know we can get worn; worn with loving others, worn with hurt, and past failures. Our hearts get heavy from the work it takes to keep on breathing. But...our hope won't fail! Let us see redemption and win; we know our struggles end and that a heart can be mended, even one that's frail and torn. We know a song can rise from the ashes of a broken life and a broken heart. And all that's dead inside can be reborn.

Restored son: Baby, you are on the winning team; restoration and redemption can be seen in our lives...a new love and a new heart. The heart knows when it can love again. Take rest and become peaceful inside as we keep on breathing. Always get up...in mind, body and spirit... then put one foot in front of the other and keep on winning, because everything broken inside can be mended as you live; you shall have victory...it's simply amazing...

Joyful son: It has been penned that your joy may be completed. This is an everlasting, settled word, a truthful and steadfast word that will never fail you or let you down. You are lavished and satiated with love and great mercies. You and I walk upon the earth...and I write to you words to encourage and strengthen you. Oh, how we love each other, calling one another "my own." May you and I be confident in the words we speak so that our joy and our lives may be complete.

Cherished son: Did you know there is a saying that you are the apple/pupil of His eye? Selah. Young man, you are truly significant in the mind of the Divine Source. My, my, my, what a wonderful love. And…You are the "apple of my eye;" and that means you are precious above all others….in my heart, mind, and soul. This private place is the place where only you are welcome to enter. Behold, what manner of caring is this that would be bestowed upon you…Your day is within your hand…create something!

Restored son: Thankful to our Creator that every answer lies within; therefore, we have hope! We are consistently connected to our Creator and the Universe with answers to our issues. You are so favored! All we need to do is ask and meditate, then we shall have the answer. My, my, you are loved with an everlasting love that will perform on your behalf because love is active. Not only do we have redemption but restoration, as the earth will answer and provide a supply for You! Stay strong and live well!

Gifted son: Surely goodness and mercy shall follow us all the days of our lives; this is what our Creator desires for us. Your best days are just ahead of you. I believe the best is saved for last in your life. You possess a blessed life and you live each day in expectation of goodness already prepared for you. You are called to be a good son, a good brother, a good husband, and a good man on Earth! And you do walk worthy of the call on your life!

Forgiven son: Some men may turn their backs, give up on us, ridicule us, embarrass us, talk about us, and hurt us as we live our life, but the mercy of our Creator prevails. Your compassion toward others should not fail but be wise. Remember, You are forgiven; therefore, we forgive. And because You make the choices in this life, You are deserving of everything good in this life and in the life to come!

Loving son: Daily you experience the loving grace of our Creator. The grace upon you is better than 1000 lives... It is my heart's pleasure to behold that ...I delightedly see your worship, I expectantly hear you pray, I excitedly hear you speak His name, and I adore you lifting up your hands in worship to Him. Like Solomon, you possess a heart of love. Like David, your loving attitude of grace toward our Creator is your life...what a wonderful life you have! Therefore, I have hope...hope of walking out our lives within grace as a sonnet of beautiful love. My guess is that you have courageously chosen me, and I choose you to love, cherish, appreciate!

Sexy son: I esteem, and honor you all the days of my life...always...

Courageous son: From within the Universe, I find you, conducting yourself in the similitude of kings. It is demonstrated in your conversation, in your spiritual walk, and in the peace in your home. A peaceful home is the right medicine after a long day, it is the right feeling after an emotional upheaval, and it is the right place to be with a man who gives love. You choose to maintain your life and living, and You are a courageous son! Along with that choice......you and your household are forever blessed!

Righteous son: Every time you are faced with any adversity or challenge—physical, mental, or emotional—use your war equipment. Enter prayer and meditation; speak good over yourself, resisting anything that would attempt to overtake you; stand firm. Stand in expectancy, stand in confidence, stand in faith. Your purpose is greater than anything that we see in this world that can come against You! You are an awe-inspiring person who has accomplished much on the Earth. It is my pleasure to know you! May love always cause you to stand; having done all... stand!

Righteous son: O Young Man, dearly beloved by the force who created You! You can stand and overcome that thing which attempts to overcome You. Peace and knowing who You are carry an emotion of passion...nothing amiss in our lives. You are a pleasing son and I just pray that you come to know this in Your life. Our Source of creation is passionate over you and the abundant life is graced for you to live…trust that word with all your heart and Your pathways will be directed toward good! Walk with confidence and be assured that all things can be restored to You!

Righteous son: O Young Man, dearly beloved son of our Creator! Today is the first day of the rest of your life! Make the most of this brand-new day filled with brand-new grace and loving kindness. Each one of us is graced and given a gift for the purpose of imparting that gift to another. If we fail to deliver the gift to another human being, we will not retain it ourselves. As the gift is imparted to another it is transferred and increases in intensity, enabling the receiver to be strengthened and in turn empowering them to give their gift. I perceive that you have many gifts and the ones I have seen demonstrated are comfort, security, hospitality, kindness, giving, open-heartedness, and an amazing gift to love deeply. I could go on but time is of the essence. I see Your works and they are good, enabling others to receive your gifts as they in turn give unto others. I have received from your heart and you have strengthened and enabled my heart to believe in love again, and in the possibility that this love can continue from earth through eternity. My love has intensified, and my viewpoint is now optimistic, and both will thrive here in the earth. Thank you for being Your created self!

Loved son: O Young Man, greatly beloved son of our Creator! You are a son! A son of love and the object of my affection. It is truly amazing how we are surrounded by love, and a love so devoted to you. Unfailing, abiding, and a lasting love all given so freely for You. And we delight in this love for it is our reason to live. Love is the main thing. Think back and always remember this…

Beloved son: You are a seeker of the heart. You walk out the precious word given. Trust that Your life is always being added to. Hope, love, joy, peace, goodness, wisdom, understanding, and a cheerful future—all these things will be added when you walk out Your calling, Your purpose. Also, you are building the necessary character to sustain your life, with traits like righteousness, right-standing, truth, honesty, justice and grace. Young Man, you are accepted, wanted and cherished. You are My beloved and in my beloved, I am well-pleased. Such a well-pleasing son you are…Such a precious love you give…such a wonderful man You have become!

Courageous son: There is nothing we endure that cannot be broken by our own dominion and rule. We are to exercise dominion over issues that attempt to rule over us. Be bold and strong, for you shall be courageous. Yay! From this moment on you shall have the victory in all situations and you shall recover ALL! This is how we live… being inspired by that anointed mind you possess! Have an awe-inspiring day.

Restored son: It thrills my heart because as you perform, you are perfected by doing. The truth is we already have inside what we need to be successful. Success is a sure thing in your life and mine.

Beloved son: I will rejoice over you with joy, love, and peace... Therefore, rejoice today for every lost or stolen thing...you are recovering all!

Blessed son: Mercy and truth will preserve your life. Oh, may we receive and give to each other compassion, hospitality, and understanding, and make certain our realities. You know the deep recesses of your unfulfilled dreams and unsatisfied hopes. Your life can be healed and restored by your thinking and doing. I desire only good for you, including me, because I am a good thing. Know yourself, do what is inside you, and become all you can to receive all that's good and right.

Courageous son: You are a strong, courageous man. Life tests our minds and our hearts with experiences. Our best days are just ahead of us as we walk into our destiny. Thank you for being courageous; spirited and gutsy. Further, you investigate the ideas of others and adopt them if truth prevails, which is portraying wisdom—a great virtue. Don't allow trials and such to move you off your firm foundation. I have your back, just as you told me that you have mine. When we have each other's backs, we become "rearguards" even when mishaps are presented…and for that I am truly grateful! Every place you go today, I am in it with you…

Restored son: Young Man, you are redeemed and restored. Our Creator takes our past, our ancient times, to renew and build up again! Our fragments are not wasted. The good work in you is faithful to bring your work to completion within you. You will encounter new mercies, and great grace at every moment. You are graced and anointed; you have an unction within to receive all things…and behold, all things become new. No matter your social, financial, emotional, physical or marital status. Our Creator is faithful to perform within your walls, within your lifetime. Our Creator is faithful to raise up your very foundation…anything that is laid waste for any amount of time…Our Creator is faithful and is the Repairer of the Breach and the Restorer…to track you within, healing paths and bring you to your desired end. It is my great pleasure to know you and I delight in praying with and for you! I am excited for you have already been restored, renewed, and repaired for glory…receive it! Great is the faithfulness of our Creator. I possess a deep and abiding love for you…have an awesome day!

Beloved son: Young Man, you are greatly accepted, and you are greatly loved by our Creator! His great love He has lavished, bestowed upon you, and that is so very exciting. Every part of your being experiences this love that is unfailing and eternal. His love repairs and rebuilds, and it is out of this great, lavished love that we love one another. Oh, greatly beloved Man, let us continually love one another as love is our highest order! He makes love what love really is. After all, everything works by His love... we need only to receive it. So be in a receiving mode for a great love in the earth...love flowing from our Creator through me. I take great pleasure in that I am preferred, the daughter of our Creator, to give you love and that you can receive it. For what on earth can be compared to a man loving a woman and a woman loving a man... endlessly? NOTHING!

Righteous son: You are anointed by your Father, our Creator, in Yeshua. You were created and inspected by Him and He called and anointed you "good." You were created to perform good works before the foundation of the earth. Now you move about the earth doing good, emulating Yeshua. You are a good brother, son, nephew, father, man, boyfriend, friend, and ultimately a good husband. You cannot be anything else except "good." That's my view of you and it won't change. I have experienced your goodness and I must testify that you do represent your Father well! You demonstrate and give good love; and that's out of a foundation of our Father's love. My, how blessed I am to know you and to share your life.... Man...goodness all around in my world (Yay!)

Sexy son: I speak to you as one loving and continuing to fall in love with learning. Young Man, you are the melody of my heart, and when we relate to each other, we make a superb harmony. This harmony is an octave of attention, including notes of delight, a double clef of affection, an octave of sharing, an octave of giving, a treble clef of tender kisses, an octave of warm caresses; blending into a heart song. Oh, may the symphony of our heart song crescendo when we turn into one. Daily may your heart scale with higher tones in the delight of blending your love and mine.

Sexy son: As the dawning of a new day, so is the continual blessing of a real love;
As the rising of the sun, so is the fire flamed of a real love;
As the intensifying view of a blue sky, so is the picturesque view of a real love;
As a star-lit night, so is the eternal beauty of a real love;
As a full moon shines, so is the fullness of a real love;
Man, you are my real love, moving about my life and making my world a unique place to live, because no one can break what we have established in our season...unconditional love!

Ceaseless will never cease,
Endless will never end,
Everlasting will always last,
Unfailing will never fail,
Unending will never end...everlasting and eternal is my love for you, Young Man!

Young Man, you are a warrior, warring over your heart and those you love.
You are a Lover, possessing a great capacity to love.
You are a Friend; your heart is knitted together with mine.
You are a Son, being who you were created to be.
Oh…how infinitely you are loved, especially by me!

Sexy son: You are the man who has been birthed into the earth. I will rejoice and be glad with You. I have tasted your love and, indeed, it is good. Every day when I awake, my heart is thrilled because You are on the planet. You are my portion, Young Man, and I have said that I would keep and honor your heart. I have delighted myself in Your love, and I believe I have the desire of my heart…You. Behold…all things have become new!

Young Man,
I thought about you a lot today; the day is very busy but I wanted you to know my thoughts!
Loving you perpetually!

Sexy son: Simply…. I miss you…I miss you….I miss you…

Sexy son: I just want to be drawn into my "safe place" and nest there…shut out all the rest of the world…in front of a warm fire. I know that this is just my desire and want and not possible now, but nonetheless, I have the pictures in my mind…. while the pictures are nice…they are just not the same as the real thing.

Sexy son: You are most welcomed…into my world!

Sexy son: I miss you like we need oxygen to breathe. But I have hope that my longing shall be fulfilled. Mercy!

Sexy son: I am enraptured…

Sexy son: I miss you like these unclothed, unrobed, dress-less trees miss their plump, vibrantly colored green leaves…those desired leaves dress them for beauty.

Sexy son: I know that you are not color blind, or blind on any level; after all…you beheld me.

Sexy son: Good morning! What a wonderful day full of new opportunities that are more precious than shiny silver, more costly than pure gold, and nothing that I remotely desire compares with the essence of You! I don't desire a person, place, or thing more than You. "No Thing" can compare with Your gracious behaviors, generosity, and giving heart toward me. And that's why I am naturally yielding to You! With the next beat of your heart…I am there… honoring You above all else. You are a blessed and favored man!

Sexy son: You really rouse me; and you have great taste…I knew I could trust you! One thing I ask, and I don't want to wait. I have a question because I just need to know: Do you miss me as I am missing you?

Nurtured son: It's another splendid day, a day we can rejoice in because we are present and healthy!

You are a heroic son! One who begins life with a rough childhood but refuses to be a product of the circumstances, and planned people are sent alongside to help. A Hero—one who looks inside themselves to gain strength from within and uses that strength to pursue and achieve, despite any fears. Young Man, YOU are a Hero! Occasionally in life, someone comes along and interconnects with the life of another, as you have mine. I pray that this truth is revealed inside You! You are a blessed and highly favored man…with whom I am well pleased!

Nurtured son: Sometimes I do become afraid. You kind of scare me a little; but I am okay now. I will be bold and brave; thank you again! Looking forward to your return!

I trust, pray, and believe that you are safe; please be safe. May the Universe that makes peace for us make peace for you today and every day of your life! Peace conveys feeling, emotion, and intent that there is nothing missing, nothing broken, nothing out of place—no sickness, only health; safety, no loss; only prosperity and completeness…simply a perfect picture of peace in your life! Live, laugh and love on purpose!

Righteous son: This is the day that our Creator has made and we will rejoice and be glad in it! No matter what has happened in your past or present, all things can be renewed. Allow the Universe to renew your mind; think of and meditate on new possibilities...restore your faith in trusting; forgive as we are forgiven...repair any mediocre relationship; as you're a righteous son, you're a caring friend, you're an empathetic brother, you're a passionate professional, and...a potentially remarkable lover. Remarkable: you have the innate capability to give and receive and to leave your legacy of kindheartedness in the earth.

Righteous son: first let me say thank you for the gift; and to let you know that what I do and the words I say are by my prayers and the meditations of my heart. You benefit from the things within my soul and my heart. While I do thank and appreciate you for your thoughtfulness, you know it's not necessary. Secondly, you get me! When you bless me or say caring, expressive words from your heart, my heart skips a beat because I know that you say words to bless me...oh, how wonderful! Remember, every good and perfect gift comes to us; it's appointed! No good thing will be withheld from you because you walk in righteousness. Lastly, I am so very grateful for YOU! Thank you again for your expression of kindness.

Nurturing son: We have another day and it's a masterpiece hand-crafted by our Creator! We will love with all of our hearts, minds, and souls, and love our neighbor accordingly. I was overjoyed with our conversation last evening and want to remind you that we possess Hope. Our hope is expanded far above anything we can imagine. Hope brings us healing for our health, hearts, and happiness. Rejoice in your Hope today and expand your imagination! Then you will find healing...which will create healthy thoughts, causing your heart to smile...you will find healing for your heart to trust again and love. Next time, you will find happiness...beyond your deferred dreams.

Sexy son: Thank you for your kindness today; it was very thoughtful and appreciated! I have truly enjoyed our time together; you are very sweet. I love your smile, your sincerity, and your affection. May we have more of these good times.

Nurturing son: We have an awesome opportunity to live in this exquisite day, brought to us by our Creator, who has skillfully crafted and fashioned you. Continue to conform your heart and thoughts in a good way. You are wonderfully blessed and favored. Feel the feeling; face all challenges and say...no fear here!

Sexy son: I will submit to whatever is in your heart to do; yes, I am like that. Plus, spending time with you face to face would be very enjoyable! What a delightful morning we have been blessed to experience! May everything you need be available and may you have wisdom beyond your years—in everything, in every moment, in every beat of your heart! Live, laugh and love on purpose! I would like to greet you in this manner each day. I hope that meets with your approval.

Nurturing son: Asking questions is how one learns and becomes proficient in applying wisdom...that is you!

Nurturing son: I just absolutely love doing "unique" things that no one else has ever done. Young Man, thank you for permitting me to be a unique person in your life. And you will discover that I will relate to you in a way that no one ever has! I am a very good journey, a life person...enjoying life, and I believe you can handle it.

Righteous son: Young Man, you are a righteous man and have great insight. I agree that there is something to be discussed because of how we all were brought up in churches and our own personal backgrounds and cultures. I don't know if each of these things can be "blended" or should be "blended" for the sake of unity. People are different for a reason. I believe we must have unity among the brothers, regardless of these things. Most of us just want to know ourselves better by the things that are within each of us. Most of us seek truth. I believe it is incumbent upon all to pray and seek truth on our journeys. Remember, there is nothing new under the sun; if the Leadership of the ancient people was successful back in their time, with different dialects, we can be successful in our time. Just my comments.

Oh, you have me figured out? Well....yes, a mess but a very good one.

Sexy son: When you take hold of my hand, there is this feeling of connection and I agree with...You!

Nurturing son: I wasn't with you for your high school days, not there for the college or audition for the NBA, not there for your military service years, not there for grad school nor the doctorate.
I wasn't there for the birth of your children; I was not with you for the challenges of your life. But I AM here now!! And it's rare in life to encounter a Hero, one who moves forward to achieve, regardless, and overcomes challenges! I AM proud of you and your life! I have encountered a hero...that is You!

Sexy son: You encouraged me to go out complete my errand. I comprehend that you like order, the appropriate arrangement of things, and out of your order comes caring, kindness and gentleness. Thank you for expanding your soul and your heart to care...yes, they do agree! Caring, kind and the gentleman that is only...You!

Sexy son: A poet who is romantic...ahhhh...breathless!
My desire for you is that you understand "I see You;"
My desire for You is that you know "You make a difference;"

My desire for You is that you experience "unfeigned caring;"
My desire for you is that you connect with me...only You!

Sexy son: We shared a hallmark moment, where I could really see into your heart. You have been looking for me for as long as I have wanted to be found by You. So precious the moment, so deep the feeling, and so fervent the desire. One moment, one instant in time, yielding the reflection where true feelings meet with true passion. Some people wait a lifetime for a moment like this! I desire more hallmark moments with...You!

Sexy son: You are like the cooling rain drops on a rainy day. You are like the wind blowing and circling on a blustery day. Yes, you are righteous in time...when my thoughts think of you, refreshing my heart...only You!

Nurturing son: You are a very caring and considerate man! It shows in your mannerisms, it shows in your decisiveness, and it shows in your willingness to "be there" ... What an awesome Creator we have who has fashioned you and your tender heart toward me. My, my...what a man—there is not one who can be compared with... You!

Nurturing son: I am indebted to the heavens eternally. My heart is filled with gratitude to the Creator. My mouth pours forth thanksgiving for all things concerning you!

You are a precious treasure...one to be cherished for a lifetime. I appreciate...You!

Nurturing son: Awake, oh heavens, Clap your hands, all the Earth. Sun, warm his pathways. Wind blow gently on his face. Stars, shine brightly to illuminate his night places. He's alive and well, walking upon the Earth. One astoundingly fine man...You!

Nurturing son: You care, and I see it even when I am not feeling well. You care, and I feel it in every embrace. You care and I hear your genuine concern...on air conditioning and car repairs. Thank you, it is so important! So, with heart-felt gratitude...Thank You!

Sexy son: As I think of you, I smile. When I am with you, I am cheered. When without you, I fondly miss you. As you think of me.... When you are with me...When you miss me...Anticipating the feelings of ...You!

Nurturing son: Say, how is your heart? Are you excited... happier...filled with anticipation? Say, how are your thoughts? Do you ponder the great possibilities of a lasting and loving relationship? Well, these are the heart-felt feelings and thoughts that I ponder...and now I have shared them with...remarkable You!

Nurturing son: I had a dream and you were in it. You were standing and gazing at me...looking pleased and delighted! You said to me, "You look like my vision of love!" Oh, wait…Oh, wait…that wasn't a dream!! You said that to me yesterday…it is immensely heart-warming to know your heart feels this way about me. Only one extraordinary…. You!

Nurturing son: A graceful pair we are. You took the time to share your professional work and your success in that work with me. I am so pleased that I could offer some comfort and encouragement to you. I feel you add value and make a difference in the lives of people…and it's not a light matter. I am so proud, and I take pleasure in meticulously focused…You!

Nurturing son: Job 8:7 – "Then what you had in the past will seem small compared with the great prosperity you'll have in the future." And today we have heard, "it matters not how you began, just finish well." I am here to encourage your heart and say, all your tomorrows look fantastic! Day after day blessing, honor, strength, and greatness pour forth on your behalf. Truly, our Creator has saved the best for last, making all of your yesterday's seem so small. Righteously, the preeminence and best man…You!

Nurturing son: Tender-hearted persons must balance their compassion with foresight and a firm kindness toward themselves, as well as toward others. This is how I see you. Very easily moved to care for and bear with those you are compassionate about. Be kind to yourself;

it's tender people who are the solid foundation of life... caring You!

Sexy son: Is it right that I miss seeing you? Is it right that I miss holding you? Is it right that I miss looking into your soulful eyes? It's more than right, it's righteous and fitting. It's moving in time and space with you in mind. It's what your eyes express when your voice is silent. It's what your arms convey when we embrace. It's what your heart refrains when we are face to face. It's admittedly... You!

Nurturing son: Much like Sinatra sang in his song *Night and Day,* no matter the distance, near or far, once you are embedded in the soul, you are always present. Incessantly in my mind, processing through...thought after thought and feeling after feeling. Never, ever weary and always anticipating. My, my, what a stimulating, thought-provoking man...You!

Nurturing son: I was meditating and being grateful. I thought, *What an amazingly awesome Creator we have! That our Creator would go into my thoughts, probe through my feelings, push past old hurts and satisfy my soul. Examine my core, and then pull out my greatest desire...pull out my unspoken requests...pull out my heart's resounding cry... and name him YOU! My, my, such a wonderfully created being ...You!*

Nurturing son: I heard the phrase, "You wear me well" and in that I take great pleasure! I trust at the remembrance of me, you wear your illuminating smile. I trust at the thought of me, you wear your pleasing feelings. I trust at the mention of me, you wear your joyful heart. I trust as you envision me, you have a renewed vigor in your step. I trust you are wearing me in thought, in word, and in your heart. And yes, I look extremely gorgeous on…You!

Nurturing son: It was very good to see you last week. Again, I am so sorry to hear of the challenges you face with your family. I know it is not easy for you and yet you persevere! Further, I pray that you are able to overcome your health challenges. Look up and don't become down-hearted. Just thinking of…You!

Nurturing son: Last night I said, "I want to make all your tomorrows amazing." I heard, "I have to go, and I will call you later." The essence of what I said was this: I want to make your lost dreams come true, I want healing and restoration of all things in you, I want to make memories with you, and I want more of you…I desire you! You said, "I have to go, and I will call you later." My mouth poured forth what my heart was saying, heartbeat by heartbeat. I desire a remarkable and intense relationship with you. You said, "I have to go, and I will call you later." I am simply trying to understand…You!

Chapter 4:
The Flame

When you are speaking and creating in your relationship, your creativity is revealing. You can create, and at the apex of my creativity I write poems and songs as I have provided below. Some will develop entrepreneurial ventures and yet others may develop in other crafts. We can develop and enhance the lives of others once we begin to operate out of our gifting that is known by our hearts. Most women never achieve this because they speak negatively or operate from hopelessness, struggling to merely survive in their relationships.

Finally, in "The Flame" there is a listing of the responses from those I have had the opportunity to speak to in a relationship. This is not for everyone you meet! You must count the cost to develop yourself, which is worth the work, and then to speak into the lives of others. Most are not going to receive what you have to say, so move on and be kind. I am confident that when you live at this level of life, you will encounter one who will love how you enhance their lives with your words building wholeness. That is where we desire to be. Their responses are what we desire to hear and what causes us to thrive in life.

The song:

"The Flame of your Love"
> Baby, your love has come into my heart
> And set my heart aflame.
> It's a precious love, a satisfying love,
> A love that will not change

> Chorus:
> There's a flame of fire called love and it is all for you, all for you.
> It cannot be quenched; it's so intense, so mesmerizing (echo... mesmerizing).
> No matter the road, no matter the cost, the flame lives on...and on... (echo... and on);
> The flame lives on and on...

> Baby, your love has come into my world
> And set my world aflame.
> It's a giving love, a fulfilling love,
> A love that will not change

> Bridge:
> The flame...it's never ceasing;
> The flame...it's never ending;
> The flame... it's unfailing;
> The flame lives on...and on; the flame lives on... and on.

Chorus:

There's a flame of fire called love and it is all for you, all for you.

It cannot be quenched; it's so intense; so mesmerizing (echo... mesmerizing).

No matter the road, no matter the cost, the flame lives on...and on... (echo... and on);

The flame lives on and on; the flame lives on and on.

The Responses:

"..that someone so unforgettable thinks I'm unforgettable too...incredible"

"Good morning, Luv. You're silent today. Anything I can do to pep you up?"

"Congratulations, Luv, you are just the complete package.... with a bonus!!! 🎓"

"Good morning, luv...I pray all is well with you and that you have a very peaceful and productive day."

"You really missed your calling. Your prose is like a multi-colored rose bouquet...beautiful and fragrant."

"Your prose continues to leave me speechless."

"My sentiments exactly"

"Thank you, it did indeed answer the question. You are a remarkable individual, and I am honored that you see me in such light."

"Tell me, have you always expressed your feelings so eloquently?"

"You must love intensely because your passion is forever evident for even the occasional visionary to see."

"I don't know how to use the fancy resources, but listen to the Dells: the love we had stays on my mind"

"Thank you for the sweet poetry. It continues to render my tongue motionless."

"You have got to get published."

"How can you see such blushing on a dark, sweet fruit? You have great vision and insight."

"You manage to write and utter the most delightful, loving and inspiring phrases and passages. That is a gift. 🌵😇😀 ❇🌲🌵📿🏺"

"You must...stand with me."

"You have the eyes and lips of a passionate lover and your words wash over one as does warm, sweetly scented oil."

"Wow... Speechless. Those are touching words that bring tears to my heart. 😊"

"Wow.... This gives me an idea for a movie."

"Gee, we are in a pensive and appreciative mood today..."

"☺ I love you.
...I love you so!!
good spicy food, even spicier woman.

Thank you, anointed Lady of YAHWEH. May his love always protect and cover you. May you always be at peace. Incredible, absolutely incredible!!!! ☺ "

"You never fail to impress me with your impeccable prose and quintessential grasp of human spiritual essence. Indeed, you are incredible."

"Somebody is in love. ☺ "

"You're a sweet and patient woman. Thank you for being with me and allowing me to experience your incredible love which our Creator has blessed you with."

"You are so beautiful to me."

"I love you for this and so much more."

"Your remarkable beauty is only surpassed by your undeniable faith. Stay beautiful, stay faithful."

"Thank you. You are a wise woman."

"Thanks, I so need those words now."

"You know the words to touch my heart."

"Thank you, sweet lady."

"Thank you, Lady Love."

"Thank you, Dorothea Edwards. You are a good and faithful servant and inspirational woman of our God. You are the fruitful land that I am to occupy. You are a fellow warrior going into the good land alongside me. You are my communicator, my ears to hear, and even my mouth to speak. I may get a little nervous, but the past is done and only serves as a platform/lesson. So, along with me, put on your full armor of our Creator and stand with me."

"I pray that love gets stronger and stronger. I wait for confirmation in all faith for his will to be done"

"Thank you, oh beautiful and virtuous child of our Creator."

"Your kind words are to my heart as sugar is to my tongue."

"Love ya intensely."

"Speechless, absolutely speechless."

"You know the words to melt a heart and keep love growing."

"The rhythm is my ribbon that ties my flowers in a bow.
The melody says darling, I love you so."

"You afford me such honor with these words. I pray that one day I will be worthy of such admiration. You are such a lovely and loving person that you set me ablaze whenever I read your words or hear your voice."

"Your prose is almost as beautiful as you are."

"Such a deeply romantic woman I have not met before.
I can never match your prose, but I can match your love.
Be blessed virtuous woman, be greatly blessed.
Powerful
Words as sweet as honey!"

"Sweet words from a sweet woman. Thank you."

"You, like our Creator, are a sonnet of beautiful love.
There has been one other courageous choice I have made.
One to love and cherish and keep in my heart forever.
Can you guess who that is?
You must...stand with me."

"I love you, yes I do; it's true. Love you, yes..."

"My First, my last, my everything...after our Creator you are..."

"You are so beautiful…to me.
A poet and beautiful songwriter… Wow
Thank you."

"Your beauty and our Creator's inspiration leave me speechless."

"Your prose is beyond anything I have ever received.
Speechless. Such beautiful prose.
You are simply incredible. Your prose is masterful, inspiring and stimulating to the spirit and soul."

"Such a sweet message serves as inspiration to be very careful 'cause I miss your tenderness and sweet words."

"I can't get you out of my mind for even an instant. I just can't believe our Creator has blessed me with you. I am profoundly blessed and grateful."

"You are so beautiful and sweet."

"Your spirit gave me a hug, and I smell your fragrance as I read your message. Thank you for that love."

"Your poetry is almost as sweet as your kiss, as tender and soft as your touch, as caressing as your love that I feel from you."

"As I am!"

"Sweet, blessed words from a sweet, lovely lady. Thank you for your prayers and thought."

"Good morning, Lady D. Be blessed, stay lovely."

"I sent a gift of gratitude to you. The gratitude is for revealing yourself to me (be bold), and for taking some of your time to hear about me and tell me about you (be brave)."

"Incredible, and thank you."

"Wow, you are truly blessed and your words appreciated. I am not as eloquent at expressing my thoughts, but may you find favor as well as blessings in all you do."

"Indeed I am intrigued. I wonder who you are."

"You're a mess. Awesome!"

"This is absolutely captivating and beautiful!"

"Pretty Lady, a kind heart is a fountain of gladness, making everything in its vicinity freshen into multiple smiles."

"Deliciously poignant and heart-warming!"

"Awesome and indistinguishable…you!"

"Very nice!"

"Very beautiful and poetic."

"Magnificent!"

"Awesome becomes you."

"You are a jewel."

"Glory!!!!"

I am Dorothea and
I love being a woman, and
I love sharing with you.
Thank you!